To

_____

From

_____

365 Day Brighteners™ *for a Special Mother*

© 2003 DaySpring Cards, Inc.
Published by Garborg's™,
a brand of DaySpring Cards, Inc.
Siloam Springs, Arkansas

Scripture quotations are from the following sources: The HOLY
BIBLE, NEW INTERNATIONAL VERSION® (niv)® © 1973,
1978, 1984 by International Bible Society. Used by permission of
Zondervan Publishing House. The Holy Bible, New Century Version
(ncv) © 1987, 1988, 1991 by Word Publishing, Dallas, Texas 75039.
Used by permission. THE MESSAGE © Eugene H. Peterson 1993,
1994, 1995. Used by permission of NavPress Publishing Group. All
rights reserved. The Living Bible (tlb) © 1971 by permission of
Tyndale House Publishers, Inc., Wheaton, IL. The New King James
Version (nkjv) © 1982, Thomas Nelson, Inc. The New Revised
Standard Version of the Bible (nrsv) © 1989 Division of Christian
Education, National Council of Churches. Used by permission of
Zondervan Publishing House.

ISBN 1-58061-576-7

Printed in China

365 DAY
BRIGHTENERS

FOR

a
Special
Mother

365 DAY
BRIGHTENERS

GARBORG'S

because every day is a gift

FOR

a
Special
Mother

$\mathcal{G}$od specializes in things fresh and firsthand. His plans for you this year may outshine those of the past....
He's preparing to fill your days with reasons to give Him praise.

Joni Eareckson Tada

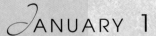

$\mathcal{J}$ANUARY 1

January 2

May God's richest blessings be upon you both today and throughout the year—and may those blessings flow through you to touch the lives of everyone you meet.

Gary Smalley & John Trent

$\mathcal{M}$ost of all the other beautiful things in life come by twos and threes, by dozens and hundreds. Plenty of roses, stars, sunsets, rainbows, brothers and sisters, aunts and cousins, comrades and friends—but only one mother in the whole world.

Kate Douglas Wiggin

$\mathcal{J}$ANUARY 3

January 4

*F*or whatever life holds for you and your family in the coming days, weave the unfailing fabric of God's Word through your heart and mind. It will hold strong, even if the rest of life unravels.

Gigi Graham Tchividjian

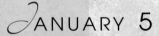

A new year can begin only because
the old year ends.

Madeleine L'Engle

But this I call to mind, and therefore I have hope:
The steadfast love of the Lord never ceases,
his mercies never come to an end;
they are new every morning;
great is your faithfulness.

Lamentations 3:21-23 NRSV

*J*ANUARY 5

January 6

Thus, simply as a little child, we learn a home is made from love. Warm as the golden hearthfire.

A child's hand in yours—what tenderness and power it arouses. You are instantly the very touchstone of wisdom and strength.

Marjorie Holmes

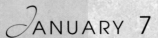

JANUARY 7

JANUARY 8

Children represent God's
most generous gift to us.

James Dobson

God knows the rhythm of my spirit
and knows my heart thoughts.
He is as close as breathing.

JANUARY 9

January 10

A good woman is hard to find,
and worth far more than diamonds.
Her husband trusts her without reserve,
and never has reason to regret it.
Never spiteful, she treats him generously
all her life long.

Proverbs 31:10-12 THE MESSAGE

$\mathcal{L}$ine by line, moment by moment,
special times are etched into our memories
in the permanent ink of everlasting love
in our relationships!

Gloria Gaither

JANUARY 12

A mother is all those wonderful things
you never outgrow your need for.

$\mathcal{W}$hen you look at your life, the greatest
happinesses are family happinesses.

Joyce Brothers

$\mathcal{J}$ANUARY 13

January 14

Maybe all I could do was mother.... And yet, why did I feel so fulfilled when I bedded down three kids between clean sheets? What if raising and instilling values in three children and turning them into worthwhile human beings would be the most important contribution I ever made in my lifetime?

Erma Bombeck

I will lie down and sleep in peace,
for you alone, O Lord,
make me dwell in safety.

Psalm 4:8 NIV

JANUARY 15

January 16

Prayer is talking and listening to God.
A prayer relationship with God is the
cornerstone of effective parenting.

Mary Manz Simon

$\mathcal{W}$hen you are dealing with a child,
keep all your wits about you
and sit on the floor.

A. O'Malley

$\mathcal{J}$ANUARY 17

January 18

Most new discoveries are suddenly-seen things that were always there.

Susanne K. Langer

*E*very day we live is a priceless gift of God, loaded with possibilities to learn something new, to gain fresh insights into His great truth.

Dale Evans Rogers

JANUARY 19

January 20

Don't worry about anything; instead, pray about everything; tell God your needs, and don't forget to thank him for his answers. If you do this, you will experience God's peace, which is far more wonderful than the human mind can understand. His peace will keep your thoughts and your hearts quiet and at rest.

Philippians 4:6-7 TLB

If you have a special need today, focus your full attention on the goodness and greatness of your Father rather than on the size of your need. Your need is so small compared to His ability to meet it.

JANUARY 21

JANUARY 22

*W*e turn not older with the years, but
newer every day.

Emily Dickinson

*T*here is no other closeness in human life like the closeness between a mother and her baby—chronologically, physically, and spiritually they are just a few heartbeats away from being the same person.

Susan Chever

JANUARY 23

January 24

Everybody can be great. Because anybody can serve. You don't have to have a college degree to serve. You don't have to make your subject and your verb agree to serve.... You only need a heart full of grace.
A soul generated by love.

Martin Luther King, Jr.

You have made known to me the path of
life; you will fill me with joy in your
presence, with eternal pleasures
at your right hand.

Psalm 16:11 NIV

JANUARY 25

January 26

It is the simple things of life that make living worthwhile, the sweet fundamental things such as love and duty, work and rest, and living close to nature.

Laura Ingalls Wilder

$\mathcal{T}$here's no vocabulary
For love within a family, love that's lived in
But not looked at,
love within the light of which
All else is seen, the love within which
All other love finds speech.

T. S. Eliot

$\mathcal{J}$ANUARY 27

January 28

*H*appiness always looks small while you hold it in your hands, but let it go, and you learn at once how big and precious it is.

Maxim Gorky

There's no love in the world
as precious as a mother's,
And no mother quite as precious as you.

JANUARY 29

JANUARY 30

*E*very single act of love
bears the imprint of God.

*My beloved friends, let us continue to love each
other since love comes from God. Everyone who
loves is born of God and experiences
a relationship with God.*

1 John 4:7 THE MESSAGE

A wonderful mother, a special friend,
that's what you've been to me...
so much a part of lovely times
I keep in memory.

*J*ANUARY 31

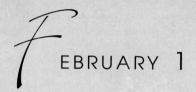

FEBRUARY 1

Kind words can be short and
easy to speak, but their echoes
are truly endless.

Mother Teresa

$\mathcal{T}$he secret of joy in work is contained in one word—excellence. To know how to do something well is to enjoy it.

Pearl S. Buck

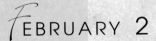

$\mathcal{F}$EBRUARY 2

FEBRUARY 3

Love is extravagant in the price
it is willing to pay, the time it is willing to
give...and the strength
it is willing to spend.

Joni Eareckson Tada

*T*rust in the Lord with all your heart
and lean not on your own understanding;
in all your ways acknowledge him,
and he will make your paths straight.

Proverbs 3:5-6 NIV

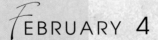

*F*EBRUARY 4

FEBRUARY 5

All mothers are rich when they love their
children.... Their love is always the
most beautiful of joys.

Maurice Maeterlinck

$\mathcal{W}$e must not, in trying to think about how we can make a big difference, ignore the small daily differences we can make which, over time, add up to big differences that we often cannot foresee.

Marian Wright Edelman

$\mathcal{F}$EBRUARY 6

FEBRUARY 7

The love of a mother is the veil
of a softer light between the heart
and the heavenly Father.

Samuel Taylor Coleridge

A mother is not a person to lean upon,
but a person to make leaning unnecessary.

Dorothy Canfield

*F*EBRUARY 8

FEBRUARY 9

Love...puts up with anything,
Trusts God always,
Always looks for the best,
Never looks back,
but keeps going to the end.
Love never dies.

1 Corinthians 13:4,7-8 THE MESSAGE

A mother is a person who if she is not there when you get home from school you wouldn't know how to get your dinner, and you wouldn't feel like eating it anyway.

February 10

FEBRUARY 11

Encouragement is being a good listener,
being positive, letting others know you
accept them for who they are.
It is offering hope, caring about the feelings
of another, understanding.

Gigi Graham Tchividjian

*W*e need time to dream, time to
remember, and time to reach the infinite.
Time to be.

Gladys Taber

*F*EBRUARY 12

*C*hildren are comforted when they're held
in their parents' arms. Hugs help
sparkle up a day.

Gary Smalley & John Trent

$\mathcal{L}$ove has its source in God,
for love is the
very essence of His being.

Kay Arthur

Follow the way of love.
1 Corinthians 14:1 NIV

$\mathcal{F}$EBRUARY 14

There is a time for risky love.
There is a time for extravagant gestures.
There is a time to pour out your affections
on one you love. And when the time
comes—seize it, don't miss it.

Max Lucado

$\mathcal{T}$here is an enduring tenderness in the love of a mother...that transcends all other affections of the heart.

Washington Irving

$\mathcal{F}$EBRUARY 16

FEBRUARY 17

The heavenly Father welcomes us with open arms and imparts to us blessing upon blessing—not because we are so good, simply because He loves us so much.

$\mathcal{W}$hat one loves in childhood
stays in the heart forever.

Mary Jo Putney

$\mathcal{F}$EBRUARY 18

FEBRUARY 19

I bless the holy name of God with all my
heart. Yes, I will bless the Lord and not
forget the glorious things he does for me....
The loving-kindness of the Lord is
from everlasting to everlasting,
to those who reverence him.

Psalm 103:1-2,17 TLB

$\mathcal{I}$f it can be verified, we don't need faith....
Faith is for that which lies on the other side
of reason. Faith is what makes life bearable,
with all its tragedies and ambiguities and
sudden, startling joys.

Madeleine L'Engle

$\mathcal{F}$EBRUARY 20

FEBRUARY 21

Once an old woman at my church said the secret is that God loves us exactly the way we are and that He loves us too much to let us stay like this. I'm just trying to trust that.

Anne Lamott

$\mathcal{W}$hat families have in common the
world around is that they are the place
where people learn who they are
and how to be that way.

Jean Illsley Clarke

$\mathcal{F}$EBRUARY 22

FEBRUARY 23

When we do the best that we can, we
never know what miracle is wrought in our
life, or in the life of another.

Helen Keller

$\mathcal{T}$he rewards of love
are always greater than the cost.

May the Lord be loyal to you in return and
reward you with many demonstrations of his
love! And I too will be kind to you because of
what you have done.

2 Samuel 2:6 TLB

$\mathcal{F}$EBRUARY 24

FEBRUARY 25

Home. A place where when
you get there, you know your heart
has been there all along.

Gloria Gaither

A mother knows the loving art
of always giving with the heart.

*F*EBRUARY 26

FEBRUARY 27

Love has been called the most effective motivational force in all the world. When love is at work in us, it is remarkable how giving and forgiving, understanding and tolerant we can be.

Charles Swindoll

God is not in the vastness of greatness. He is hid in the vastness of smallness. He is not in the general. He is in the particular.

Pearl S. Buck

FEBRUARY 28

FEBRUARY 29

Who understands much,
forgives much.

Madame de Staël

Be kind to each another, tenderhearted,
forgiving one another;
just as God has forgiven you.

Ephesians 4:32 TLB

*N*o one ever outgrows
the need for a mother's love.

Janette Oke

*M*ARCH 1

MARCH 2

*E*veryone was meant to share
God's all-abiding love and care;
He saw that we would need to know
a way to let these feelings show....
So God made hugs.

Jill Wolf

Courage doesn't always roar. Sometimes courage is the little voice at the end of the days that says...I'll try again tomorrow.

MARCH 3

MARCH 4

Half the joy of life is in little things taken
on the run. Let us run if we must—even the
sands do that—but let us keep our hearts
young and our eyes open that nothing worth
our while shall escape us. And everything
is worth its while if we only
grasp it and its significance.

Victor Cherbuliez

$\mathcal{A}$s high as heaven is over the earth,
so strong is his love to those who fear him....
As parents feel for their children,
God feels for those who fear him.

Psalm 103:11,13 THE MESSAGE

$\mathcal{M}$ARCH 5

MARCH 6

*E*very day in a life fills the whole life
with expectation and memory.

C. S. Lewis

$\mathcal{I}$t isn't what happens; it's how you deal with it that's important.

MARCH 7

MARCH 8

The most important thing she'd learned
over the years was that there was no way to
be a perfect mother and a million
ways to be a good one.

Jill Churchill

$\mathcal{T}$each me, Father, to value each day,
to live, to love, to laugh, to play.

Kathi Mills

$\mathcal{M}$ARCH 9

MARCH 10

$\mathcal{L}$et us not become weary in doing good,
for at the proper time we will reap a harvest
if we do not give up.

*Therefore, as we have opportunity,
let us do good to all people.*

Galatians 6:9-10 NIV

*A*h! there is nothing like staying at home,
for real comfort.

Jane Austen

*M*ARCH 11

Some emotions don't make a lot of noise.
It's hard to hear pride. Caring is real faint—
like a heartbeat. And pure love—
why, some days it's so quiet,
you don't even know it's there.

Erma Bombeck

*W*e shape our dwellings, and afterwards
our dwellings shape us.

Winston Churchill

MARCH 13

MARCH 14

Motherhood: If it was going to be easy,
it never would have started
with something called labor.

Barbara Johnson

God rewards a mother's love with the
blessing of her children's love.

Her children arise and call her blessed.

Proverbs 31:28 NIV

MARCH 15

MARCH 16

Peace is the center of the atom, the core
Of quiet within the storm....
Peace is not placidity: peace is
The power to endure the megatron of pain
With joy, the silent thunder of release,
The ordering of Love.
Peace is the atom's start,
The primal image:
God within the heart.

Madeleine L'Engle

$\mathcal{S}$o many things we love are you, I can't seem to explain except by little things, but flowers and beautiful handmade things—small stitches. So much of our reading and thinking, so many sweet customs and so much of our...well, religion. It is all you.

Anne Morrow Lindbergh

$\mathcal{M}$ARCH 17

$\mathcal{M}$ARCH 18

$\mathcal{L}$ove is the seed of all hope. It is the enticement to trust, to risk, to try, to go on.

Gloria Gaither

$\mathcal{Y}$ou who have received so much love, show your love by protecting the sacredness of life. The sacredness of life is one of the greatest gifts that God has given us.

Mother Teresa

$\mathcal{M}$ARCH 19

ℳarch 20

*J*ust to be is a blessing.
Just to live is holy.

Abraham Joshua Heschel

God's blessing makes life rich;
nothing we do can improve on God.

Proverbs 10:22 THE MESSAGE

$\mathcal{W}$e should all have one person who knows how to bless us despite the evidence.

Phyllis Theroux

$\mathcal{M}$ARCH 21

MARCH 22

The very word "motherhood" has an emotional depth and significance few terms have. It bespeaks nourishment and safety and sheltering arms.

Marjorie Holmes

A mother understands
what a child does not say.

Jewish Proverb

*M*ARCH 23

MARCH 24

Lovely, complicated wrappings
Sheath the gift of one-day-more;
Breathless, I untie the package—
Never lived this day before!

Gloria Gaither

$\mathcal{T}$his is the day the Lord has made.
We will rejoice and be glad in it.

Psalm 118:24 TLB

$\mathcal{M}$ARCH 25

MARCH 26

You never get over bein' a child
long's you have a mother to go to.

Sarah Orne Jewett

*O*nce we discover how to appreciate the timeless values in our daily experiences, we can enjoy the best things in life.

Harry Hepner

*M*ARCH 27

MARCH 28

Those who bring sunshine to the lives of
others cannot keep it from themselves.

Sir James M. Barrie

$\mathcal{G}$ive a little love to a child and you get a great deal back.

John Ruskin

$\mathcal{M}$ARCH 29

MARCH 30

I tell you the truth, you must accept the
kingdom of God as if you were a little child,
or you will never enter it.

Mark 10:15 NCV

When we recall the past, we usually find that it is the simplest things—not the great occasions—that in retrospect give off the greatest glow of happiness.

Bob Hope

MARCH 31

A mother's arms are made of tenderness
and children sleep soundly in them.

Victor Hugo

*W*hen God thought of mother, He must have laughed with satisfaction—so rich, so deep, so divine, so full of soul, power, and beauty, was the conception!

Henry Ward Beecher

*A*PRIL 2

$\mathcal{A}$PRIL 3

$\mathcal{I}$t is a special gift to be able to view the world through the eyes of a child.

$\mathcal{J}$esus cannot forget us; we have been
graven on the palms of His hands.

Lois Picillo

I will not forget you.
See, I have inscribed you
on the palms of my hands.

Isaiah 49:15, 16 NRSV

$\mathcal{A}$PRIL 4

$\mathcal{A}$PRIL 5

$\mathcal{H}$ow dear to the heart are the scenes of
my childhood, when fond recollection
presents them to view.

Samuel Woodworth

*M*other is the name for God in the lips
and hearts of little children.

William Makepeace Thackeray

*A*PRIL 6

April 7

Having someone who understands is a great blessing for ourselves. Being someone who understands is a great blessing to others.

Janette Oke

*E*ven when freshly washed and
relieved of all obvious confections,
children tend to be sticky.

F. Lebowitz

*A*PRIL 8

$\mathcal{A}$PRIL 9

$\mathcal{D}$on't you see that children
are God's best gift?
the fruit of the womb
his generous legacy?

Psalm 127:3 THE MESSAGE

A mother's love for the child of her body differs essentially from all other affection, and burns with so steady and clear a flame that it appears like the one unchangeable thing in this earthly mutable life.

W. H. Hudson

*A*PRIL 10

$\mathcal{A}$PRIL 11

$\mathcal{W}$hen you have laboriously
accomplished your daily task, go to sleep in
peace.
God is awake.

Victor Hugo

*I*t ought, therefore, to enter into the
domestic policy of every parent, to make her
children feel that home
is the happiest place in the world...
this delicious home-feeling is one of the
choicest gifts a parent can bestow.

Beeton's Book of Household Management

*A*PRIL 12

APRIL 13

$\mathcal{L}$ove is an act of endless forgiveness,
a tender look which becomes a habit.

Peter Ustinov

*T*he wisdom that comes from heaven is
first of all pure and full of quiet gentleness.

James 3:17 TLB

*A*PRIL 14

APRIL 15

Stay, stay at home, my heart, and rest;
Homekeeping hearts are happiest.

Longfellow

$\mathcal{T}$he God who created, names, and
numbers the stars in the heavens also
numbers the hairs of my head.... He pays
attention to very big things and to very small
ones. What matters to me matters to Him,
and that changes my life.

Elisabeth Elliot

$\mathcal{A}$PRIL 16

$\mathcal{A}$PRIL 17

$\mathcal{G}$od, help me to be honest so my children
will learn honesty.
Help me to be kind so my children
will learn kindness.
Help me to be faithful so my children
will learn faith.
Help me to love so that my children
will be loving.

Marian Wright Edelman

$\mathcal{L}$ift up your eyes. Your heavenly Father waits to bless you—in inconceivable ways to make your life what you never dreamed it could be.

Anne Ortlund

$\mathcal{A}$PRIL 18

APRIL 19

Do you want to stand out? Then step down. Be a servant. If you puff yourself up, you'll get the wind knocked out of you. But if you're content to simply be yourself, your life will count for plenty.

Matthew 23:11-12 THE MESSAGE

$\mathcal{T}$he real secret behind motherhood...love,
the thing that money can't buy.

Anna Crosby

$\mathcal{A}$PRIL 20

Call it clan, call it a network, call it a tribe, call it a family. Whatever you call it, whoever you are, you need one.

Jane Howard

$\mathcal{W}$hen our relationships are born in the heart of God, they bring out the best in us, for they are nurtured by love.

Don Lessin

$\mathcal{A}$PRIL 22

APRIL 23

$\mathcal{M}$other love is the fuel that enables a normal human being to do the impossible.

Marion C. Garretty

*P*ut God in charge of your work,
then what you've planned will take place....
We plan the way we want to live,
but only God makes us able to live it.

Proverbs 16:3,9 THE MESSAGE

*A*PRIL 24

April 25

God takes care of His own. He knows our needs. He anticipates our crises. He is moved by our weaknesses. He stands ready to come to our rescue. And at just the right moment He steps in and proves Himself as our faithful heavenly Father.

Charles Swindoll

*T*radition gives us a sense of solidarity and
roots, a knowing there are some
things one can count on.

Gloria Gaither

*A*PRIL 26

Families give us many things—love and meaning, purpose and an opportunity to give, and a sense of humor.

*F*aith in small things has repercussions that ripple all the way out. In a huge, dark room a little match can light up the place.

Joni Eareckson Tada

*A*PRIL 28

April 29

God's love...is ever and always,
eternally present to all who fear him,
Making everything right for them
and their children.

Psalm 103:17 THE MESSAGE

I once asked one of my smaller children what he thought a home was and he replied, "It's a place where you come in out of the rain."

Gigi Graham Tchividjian

*A*PRIL 30

May 1

May you wake each day with God's blessings and sleep each night in His keeping. And as you grow older, may you always walk in His tender care.

$\mathcal{A}$ smile takes but a moment, but its effects sometimes last forever.

J. E. Smith

$\mathcal{M}$ AY 2

$\mathcal{M}$AY 3

$\mathcal{Y}$ou who have received so much love share it with others. Love others the way that God has loved you, with tenderness.

Mother Teresa

$\mathcal{M}$ ay the Lord richly bless both you and your children. Yes, Jehovah who made heaven and earth will personally bless you!

Psalm 115:14-15 TLB

$\mathcal{M}$ AY 4

May 5

Our sweetest experiences of affection are meant to point us to that realm which is the real and endless home of the heart.

Henry Ward Beecher

Slow down awhile! Push aside the press
of the immediate. Take time today,
if only for a moment, to lovingly encourage
each one in your family.

Gary Smalley & John Trent

MAY 6

MAY 7

Yesterday is already a dream and tomorrow is only a vision. But today well lived makes every yesterday a dream of happiness and every tomorrow a vision of hope.

$\mathcal{L}$ife is not intended to be simply a round of work, no matter how interesting and important that work may be. A moment's pause to watch the glory of a sunrise or a sunset is soul satisfying, while a bird's song will set the steps to music all day long.

Laura Ingalls Wilder

$\mathcal{M}$AY 8

MAY 9

Those who hope in the Lord
will renew their strength.
They will soar on wings like eagles;
they will run and not grow weary,
they will walk and not be faint.

Isaiah 40:31 NIV

$\mathcal{M}$otherhood...is the only love I have known that is expansive and that could have stretched to contain with equal passion more than one object.

Erma Kurtz

$\mathcal{M}$AY 10

MAY 11

God makes our lives a medley of joy and tears, hope and help, love and encouragement.

On Mother's Day, I think moms should be
able to wake up and say to themselves:
I'm a domestic goddess!

Barbara Johnson

MAY 12

May 13

Mother love makes a woman
more vulnerable than any other
creature on earth.

Pam Brown

$\mathcal{W}$hat a wonderful God we have—
he is...the source of every mercy,
and the one who so wonderfully
comforts and strengthens us.

2 Corinthians 1:3-4 TLB

$\mathcal{M}$AY 14

May 15

Other things may change us, but we start and end with the family.

Anthony Brandt

$\mathcal{E}$ach dawn holds a new hope for a new
plan, making the start of each day
the start of a new life.

Gina Blair

$\mathcal{M}$AY 16

May 17

All God's glory and beauty come from within, and there He delights to dwell. His visits there are frequent, His conversation sweet, His comfort refreshing, His peace passing all understanding.

Thomas à Kempis

*I*f a child is to keep his inborn sense of wonder...he needs the companionship of at least one adult who can share it, rediscovering with him the joy, excitement, and mystery of the world we live in.

Rachel Carson

*M*AY 18

May 19

Where your treasure is,
there your heart will be also.

Matthew 6:21 NIV

*T*he surest way to be happy is to seek happiness for others.

Martin Luther King, Jr.

*M*AY 20

May 21

Mothers are lots of things—doctors, writers, lawyers, gardeners, actresses, cooks, police officers, sometimes even truck drivers. And mothers. Thank you, Lord.

Madeleine L'Engle

$\mathcal{R}$emember that you are needed. There is at least one important work to be done that will not be done unless you do it.

Charles Allen

$\mathcal{M}$AY 22

May 23

If God is here for us and not elsewhere,
then in fact this place is holy and
this moment is sacred.

Isabel Anders

A good laugh is as good
as a prayer sometimes.

Lucy Maud Montgomery

He will yet fill your mouth with laughter
and your lips with shouts of joy.

Job 8:21 NIV

*M*AY 24

May 25

*W*here your pleasure is, there is your treasure; where your treasure, there your heart; where your heart, there your happiness.

Augustine

$\mathcal{W}$e can change the world inside our own houses. Take the gift of this moment and make something beautiful of it. Few worthwhile experiences just happen; memories are made on purpose.

Gloria Gaither

$\mathcal{M}$AY 26

May 27

The gift of praise is the best gift you can give your child, any time of the year.

$\mathcal{W}$e are not called by God to do
extraordinary things, but to do ordinary
things with extraordinary love.

Jean Vanier

$\mathcal{M}$AY 28

May 29

May the Lord bless and protect you; may the Lord's face radiate with joy because of you; may he be gracious to you, show you his favor, and give you his peace.

Numbers 6:24-26 TLB

$\mathcal{L}$ove is that condition in which the
happiness of another person
is essential to your own.

Robert Heinlein

$\mathcal{M}$AY 30

May 31

I see children as kites. You spend a lifetime trying to get them off the ground. You run with them until you're both breathless. They crash...you add a longer tail...you patch and comfort, adjust and teach. You watch them lifted by the wind and assure them that someday they'll fly.

Erma Bombeck

A ship in the harbor is safe,
but that is not what ships are built for.

JUNE 1

JUNE 2

Just as there comes a warm sunbeam into
every cottage window,
so comes a love—born of God's care for
every separate need.

Nathaniel Hawthorne

Embrace this God-life. Really embrace it, and nothing will be too much for you.... That's why I urge you to pray for absolutely everything, ranging from small to large. Include everything as you embrace this God-life, and you'll get God's everything.

Mark 11:22-24 THE MESSAGE

JUNE 3

JUNE 4

Love comes when we take the time to
understand and care for another person.

Janette Oke

$\mathcal{M}$oments spent listening, talking, playing, and sharing together may be the most important times of all.

Gloria Gaither

$\mathcal{J}$UNE 5

JUNE 6

When we call on God, He bends down
His ear to listen, as a father bends down to
listen to his little child.

Elizabeth Charles

$\mathcal{H}$ome is the one place in all this world
where hearts are sure of each other.

Frederick W. Robertson

$\mathcal{J}$UNE 7

JUNE 8

Because the Lord is my Shepherd, I have everything I need! He lets me rest in meadow grass and leads me beside the quiet streams. He gives me new strength. He helps me do what honors him the most.

Psalm 23:1-3 TLB

*W*hat parent can tell when some fragmentary gift of knowledge or wisdom will enrich her children's lives? Or how a small seed of information passed from one generation to another may generate a new science, a new industry—a seed which neither the giver nor the receiver can truly evaluate at the time.

Helena Rubenstein

JUNE 9

JUNE 10

God's heart is the most sensitive and tender of all. No act goes unnoticed, no matter how insignificant or small.

Richard J. Foster

$\mathcal{T}$here is no duty we so much underrate as
the duty of being happy.
By being happy we sow anonymous benefits
upon the world.

Robert Louis Stevenson

JUNE 11

JUNE 12

It is a fine seasoning for joy to
think of those we love.

Molière

*H*ome is the definition of God.

Emily Dickinson

God is our refuge and strength,
a very present help in trouble.
Therefore we will not fear.

Psalm 46:1-2 KJV

*J*UNE 13

June 14

The measure of your real success
is one you cannot spend—
it's the way your child describes you
when talking to a friend.

Martin Baxbaum

Cherish your human connections: your relationships with friends and family.

Barbara Bush

JUNE 15

June 16

Mother had a thousand thoughts to get through within a day, and...most of these were about avoiding disaster.

Natalie Kusz

*C*haracter is what emerges from all the little things you were too busy to do yesterday, but did anyway.

Mignon McLaughlin

*J*UNE 17

June 18

i bless the holy name of God with all my
heart.... He surrounds me with
loving-kindness and tender mercies. He fills
my life with good things! My youth is
renewed like the eagle's!

Psalm 103:1,4-5 TLB

*J*oy is the holy fire that keeps our purpose
warm and our intelligence aglow.

Helen Keller

*J*UNE 19

June 20

$\mathcal{M}$y precious family and friends have
taught me that joy and sorrows,
storms and sunshine, tears and laughter
are all part of living—and the sun does shine
on the other side.

Margaret Jensen

$\mathcal{L}$ove is the true means by which the world is enjoyed: our love to others, and others' love to us.

Thomas Traherne

$\mathcal{J}$UNE 21

JUNE 22

Only He who created the wonders of the
world entwines hearts in an eternal way.

$\mathcal{T}$he Lord will guide you always; he will
satisfy your needs in a sun-scorched land....
You will be like a well-watered garden,
like a spring whose waters never fail.

Isaiah 58:11 NIV

JUNE 23

God has a purpose for your life and no
one else can take your place.

*T*he joy of motherhood:
What a woman experiences when
all the children are finally in bed.

Barbara Johnson

*J*UNE 25

June 26

*I*f we are cheerful and contented, all nature smiles...the flowers are more fragrant, the birds sing more sweetly, and the sun, moon, and stars all appear more beautiful and seem to rejoice with us.

Orison Swett Marden

$\mathcal{T}$radition is a form of promise from parent to child. It's a way to say, "I love you," "I'm here for you," and "Some things will not change."

Lynn Ludwick

$\mathcal{J}$UNE 27

June 28

So, chosen by God for this new life of love, dress in the wardrobe God picked out for you: compassion, kindness, humility, quiet strength, discipline.... Forgive as quickly and completely as the Master forgave you. And regardless of what else you put on, wear love. It's your basic, all-purpose garment. Never be without it.

Colossians 3:12-14 THE MESSAGE

The wind rushing through the grass, the thrush in the treetops, and children tumbling in senseless mirth stir in us a bright faith in life.

Donald Culross Peattie

JUNE 29

JUNE 30

A mother's love is the heart of the home.
Her children's sense of security and
self-worth are found there.

The light of God surrounds me,
The love of God enfolds me,
The presence of God protects me,
God is always with me.

July 1

*G*od invented parenthood. He is for us.
He is for each of our children. He is
champion of their lives, their years,
their health, their calling,
and their eternal destiny.

Ralph T. Mattson & Thom Black

A good laugh is sunshine in a house.

William Makepeace Thackeray

A cheerful heart is good medicine.

Proverbs 17:22 NIV

JULY 3

JULY 4

Nothing is so strong as gentleness, and
nothing so gentle as real strength.

Francis de Sales

$\mathcal{A}$n infinite God can give all of Himself to
each of His children. He does not
distribute Himself that each may
have a part, but to each one
He gives all of Himself.

A. W. Tozer

$\mathcal{J}$ULY 5

July 6

But every house where Love abides
And Friendship is a guest,
Is surely home, and home sweet home,
For there the heart can rest.

Henry Van Dyke

*W*hat we do is less than a drop in the ocean. But if that drop were missing, the ocean would lack something.

Mother Teresa

JULY 7

July 8

May the God of hope fill you with all joy
and peace in believing, that you
may abound in hope.

Romans 15:13 NKJV

$\mathcal{L}$oving and being loved is the greatest of human joys, the ultimate human experience.

Edward E. Ford

JULY 9

July 10

Hold fast your dreams!
Within your heart
Keep one still, secret spot
Where dreams may go
And, sheltered so,
May thrive and grow.

Louise Driscoll

$\mathcal{G}$etting things accomplished isn't nearly as important as taking time for love.

Janette Oke

$\mathcal{J}$ULY 11

Making the decision to have a child—
it's momentous. It is to decide forever
to have your heart go walking around
outside your body.

Elizabeth Stone

$\mathcal{H}$ome is where one starts from.

T. S. Eliot

You should be like one big happy family,
full of sympathy toward each other,
loving one another with tender hearts
and humble minds.

1 Peter 3:8 TLB

$\mathcal{J}$ULY 13

July 14

They might not need me; but they might.
I'll let my head be just in sight;
A smile as small as mine might be
Precisely their necessity.

Emily Dickinson

*H*appiness comes of the capacity to feel deeply, to enjoy simply, to think freely, to risk life, to be needed.

Storm Jameson

*J*ULY 15

July 16

There is no innocent sleep so innocent as
sleep shared between a woman and a child,
the little breath hurrying beside the longer,
as a child's foot runs.

Alice Meynel

I long to accomplish a great and noble task,
but it is my chief duty to accomplish
humble tasks as though they were
great and noble.

Helen Keller

*J*ULY 17

July 18

Charm can mislead and beauty soon fades.
The woman to be admired and praised
is the woman who lives in the Fear-of-God.

Proverbs 31:30 THE MESSAGE

$\mathcal{W}$e all mold one another's dreams. We all hold each other's fragile hopes in our hands. We all touch others' hearts.

$\mathcal{J}$ULY 19

July 20

God is every moment totally aware of each one of us. Totally aware in intense concentration and love.... No one passes through any area of life, happy or tragic, without the attention of God.

Eugenia Price

I have finally come to understand that it is only in the silence that I can hear the story of my life and the voice of God talking to me through the telling of it.

Peggy Benson

JULY 21

July 22

Children help us rediscover the joy,
excitement, and mystery
of the world we live in.

The eternal God is your refuge,
and underneath are the everlasting arms.

Deuteronomy 33:27 TLB

JULY 23

July 24

The happiness of life is made up of little things—a smile, a hug, a moment of shared laughter.

$\mathcal{T}$he most important things
in your home are people.

Barbara Johnson

$\mathcal{J}$ULY 25

July 26

Who ran to help me when I fell,
And would some pretty story tell,
Or kiss the place to make it well?
My Mother.

Ann Taylor

I have found that I often see God more clearly when I allow myself...free-spirited play, for my spiritual insight is sharpened.

Lois Mowday Rabey

JULY 27

July 28

For God is sheer beauty,
all-generous in love,
loyal always and ever.

Psalm 100:5 THE MESSAGE

*N*o language can express the power and beauty and heroism and majesty of a mother's love.

Edwin Hubbell

*J*ULY 29

July 30

The focus of our day is the dinner table....
When the children were in school I didn't
care what time we ate dinner as long as we
ate it together.... This was the time the
community (except for very small babies)
gathered together, when I saw most clearly
illustrated the beautiful principle
of unity in diversity.

Madeleine L'Engle

Try to see the beauty "in your own backyard," to notice the miracles of everyday life, to see the specialness of your own children, and to value the treasure of a good marriage.

Gloria Gaither

JULY 31

AUGUST 1

Thank goodness for August—the time to lie back and wallow in the knowledge that there is absolutely no occasion to rise to.

Barbara Johnson

The only footprints on the sands of time
that will really last, are the ones
made after knee prints!

C. W. Renwick

Pray without ceasing.

1 Thessalonians 5:17 KJV

AUGUST 2

AUGUST 3

What feeling is so nice as a child's hand in yours? So small, so soft and warm, like a kitten huddling in the shelter of your clasp.

Marjorie Holmes

*A*ll the great blessings of my life
Are present in my thoughts today.

Phoebe Cary

AUGUST 4

August 5

God loves us; not because we are lovable
but because He is love, not because
He needs to receive but because
He delights to give.

C. S. Lewis

Little drops of water,
Little grains of sand,
Make the mighty ocean,
And the pleasant land.
Thus the little minutes,
Humble though they be,
Make the mighty ages
Of eternity.

Julia Fletcher Carney

August 6

AUGUST 7

I love these little people; and it is not a
slight thing when they, who are so
fresh from God, love us.

Charles Dickens

Taking the child in his arms
[Jesus] said to them, "Anyone who welcomes
a little child like this in my name
is welcoming me."

Mark 9:37 TLB

$\mathcal{W}$here we love is home, home that our feet may leave, but not our hearts.

Oliver Wendell Holmes

$\mathcal{A}$UGUST 8

AUGUST 9

Who is queen of baby land?
Mother kind and sweet,
And her love, born above,
Guides the little feet.

The ultimate goal of parenthood is to allow
your children to become the persons God
intended them to be.

AUGUST 10

August 11

I looked on child rearing not only as a work of love and duty but as a profession that was fully as interesting and challenging as any honorable profession in the world and one that demanded the best that I could bring to it.

Rose Kennedy

$\mathcal{T}$o a child, love is spelled t-i-m-e.

Then Jesus took the children in his arms, put his hands on them, and blessed them.

Mark 10:16 NCV

$\mathcal{A}$UGUST 12

AUGUST 13

True worth is in *being*, not *seeming*—
In doing, each day that goes by,
Some little good—not in dreaming
Of great things to do by and by.

Alice Cary

$\mathcal{G}$od will never, never, never let us down if we have faith and put our trust in Him.

Mother Teresa

$\mathcal{A}$UGUST 14

August 15

The best and most beautiful things in the world cannot be seen or even touched. They must be felt with the heart.

Helen Keller

*I*f facts are the seeds that later produce
knowledge and wisdom, then the emotions
and the impressions of the senses are the
fertile soil in which the seeds must grow.

Rachel Carson

August 16

AUGUST 17

The Lord says, "As surely as I live,
your children will be like jewels
that a bride wears proudly."

Isaiah 49:18 NCV

There is nothing more thrilling in this world, I think, than having a child that is yours, and yet is mysteriously a stranger.

Agatha Christie

AUGUST 18

AUGUST 19

God bless my mother, all that I am or ever hope to be I owe to her.

Abraham Lincoln

*F*irst keep peace within yourself, then you can also bring peace to others.

Thomas à Kempis

*A*UGUST 20

AUGUST 21

*E*very material goal, even if it is met,
will pass away. But the heritage
of children is timeless. Our children
are our messages to the future.

Billy Graham

$\mathcal{Y}$our thoughts—how rare, how beautiful!
God, I'll never comprehend them!
I couldn't even begin to count them—
any more than I could count
the sand of the sea.
Oh, let me rise in the morning
and live always with you!

Psalm 139:17-18 THE MESSAGE

$\mathcal{A}$UGUST 22

AUGUST 23

A young child, a fresh, uncluttered mind,
a world before him—to what treasures will
you lead him?

Gladys M. Hunt

*U*sually parents who are lucky in the kind
of children they have,
have children who are lucky
in the kind of parents they have.

*A*UGUST 24

August 25

Happiness consists not in having much,
but in being content with little.

Countess of Blessington

When things go wrong,
as they sometimes will,
When the road you're trudging
seems all uphill,
When the funds are low
and the debts are high,
And you want to smile,
but you have to sigh,
When care is pressing you down a bit,
Rest, if you must—but don't you quit!

August 26

$\mathcal{A}$UGUST 27

$\mathcal{E}$nthusiasm is a divine possession.

Margaret E. Sangster

*She is clothed with strength
and dignity; she can laugh
at the days to come.*

Proverbs 31:25 NIV

God has a thousand ways
Where I can see not one;
When all my means have reached their end
Then His have just begun.

Esther Guyot

AUGUST 28

AUGUST 29

The loveliest masterpiece of the heart of
God is the heart of a mother.

Thérèse of Lisieux

*C*leaning your house
while your kids are still growing
is like shoveling the walk
before it stops snowing.

Phyllis Diller

*A*UGUST 30

AUGUST 31

Children seldom misquote you. They more often repeat word for word what you shouldn't have said.

Mae Maloo

*F*or I will give you abundant water for your thirst.... And I will pour out my Spirit and my blessings on your children.

Isaiah 44:3 TLB

SEPTEMBER 1

SEPTEMBER 18

She who would have beautiful roses in
her garden must have beautiful roses
in her heart.

Sir Reynolds Hole

$\mathcal{L}$ove...it begins with a moment that grows
richer and brighter...
and becomes a lifetime of joy.

SEPTEMBER 19

September 20

The secret of life is that all we have
and are is a gift of grace to be shared.

Lloyd John Ogilvie

These are the children God has given me.
God has been good to me.

Genesis 33:5 NCV

SEPTEMBER 21

SEPTEMBER 22

A mother is...one who can take
the place of all others, but whose place no
one else can take.

Gaspard Mermillod

I wish you love and strength
and faith and wisdom,
Goods, gold enough
to help some needy one.
I wish you songs,
but also blessed silence,
And God's sweet peace
when every day is done.

Dorothy Nell McDonald

SEPTEMBER 23

September 24

Fill the cup of happiness for others,
and there will be enough overflowing to
fill yours to the brim.

Rose Pastor Stokes

A kind heart is a fountain of gladness,
making everything in its vicinity
freshen into smiles.

Washington Irving

SEPTEMBER 25

September 26

A family is a little world created by love.

Love...believes all things, hopes all things.

1 Corinthians 13:4,7 NKJV

It doesn't take monumental feats to make the world a better place. It can be as simple as letting someone go ahead of you in a grocery line.

Barbara Johnson

S̶EPTEMBER 27

SEPTEMBER 28

*I*f it weren't for the last minute,
nothing would get done.

The ordinary acts we practice every day at home are of more importance to the soul than their simplicity might suggest.

Thomas Moore

SEPTEMBER 29

SEPTEMBER 30

Reach high, for stars lie
hidden in your soul.
Dream deep, for every dream
precedes the goal.

Pamela Vaull Starr

$\mathcal{W}$hatever is true, whatever is noble,
whatever is right, whatever is pure,
whatever is lovely, whatever is admirable—
if anything is excellent or praiseworthy—
think about such things.

Philippians 4:8 NIV

$\mathcal{O}$CTOBER 1

OCTOBER 2

The goodness of God is infinitely more
wonderful than we will ever
be able to comprehend.

A. W. Tozer

$\mathscr{I}$f there be one thing pure...that can endure, when all else passes away... it is a mother's love.

Marchioness de Spadara

$\mathscr{O}$CTOBER 3

OCTOBER 4

When we make ourselves vulnerable, we do open ourselves to pain, sometimes excruciating pain. The more people we love, the more we are liable to be hurt....
But our souls do not grow if we insulate ourselves from pain.

Madeleine L'Engle

*G*od pardons like a mother who kisses the offense into everlasting forgetfulness.

Henry Ward Beecher

OCTOBER 5

October 6

Every good and perfect gift is from above, coming down from the Father of the heavenly lights, who does not change like shifting shadows.

James 1:17 NIV

The uncertainties of the present always give way to the enchanted possibilities of the future.

Gelsey Kirkland

OCTOBER 7

OCTOBER 8

We see those we love in every sunrise and in every sunset, in every tree and in every flower.

To love by freely giving is its own reward.
To be possessed by love and to in turn give
love away is to find the secret
of abundant life.

Gloria Gaither

*O*CTOBER 9

OCTOBER 10

There is no need to plead that the love of God shall fill our hearts as though He were unwilling to fill us.... Love is pressing around us on all sides like air. Cease to resist it and instantly love takes possession.

Amy Carmichael

$\mathcal{B}$e glad for all God is planning for you.
Be patient...and prayerful always.

Romans 12:12 TLB

$\mathcal{O}$CTOBER 11

OCTOBER 12

Stories first heard at a mother's knee are never wholly forgotten—a little spring that never quite dries up.

G. Ruffini

To speak gratitude is courteous and
pleasant, to enact gratitude
is generous and noble,
but to live gratitude is to touch Heaven.

Johannes A. Gaertner

OCTOBER 13

OCTOBER 14

Real love loves for love's sake and not
because the loved one is lovable.

Eugenia Price

A mother who walks with God knows He
only asks her to take care of the possible and
to trust Him with the impossible.

Ruth Bell Graham

*O*CTOBER 15

OCTOBER 16

Love each other as God loves you, with
an intense and particular love.

Mother Teresa

A new command I give you:
Love one another. As I have
loved you, so you must love one another.

John 13:34 NIV

$\mathcal{L}$ove is never lost. If not reciprocated,
it will flow back and soften
and purify the heart.

Washington Irving

$\mathcal{O}$CTOBER 17

OCTOBER 18

The only time a woman wishes she were a
year older is when she is carrying a baby.

M. Marsh

"*Hope*" is the thing with feathers
That perches in the soul,
And sings the tune without the words,
And never stops at all.

Emily Dickinson

OCTOBER 19

OCTOBER 20

Remember—the root word of humble and human is the same: humus; earth. We are dust. We are created; it is God who made us and not we ourselves.

Madeleine L'Engle

$\mathcal{M}$y God is changeless in his love for me,
and he will come and help me.

Psalm 59:10 TLB

$\mathcal{O}$CTOBER 21

I am beginning to learn that it is the sweet,
simple things of life which are
the real ones after all.

Laura Ingalls Wilder

$\mathcal{T}$o be rooted is perhaps the most important and least recognized need of the human soul.

Simone Weil

$\mathcal{O}$CTOBER 23

OCTOBER 24

On other people you might bestow rich gifts, but to me you have given the greatest gift of all. You gave me the gift of yourself.

$\mathcal{T}$hank the Lord, it is His love that arranges our tomorrows—and we may be certain that whatever tomorrow brings, His love sent it our way.

Charles Swindoll

$\mathcal{O}$CTOBER 25

OCTOBER 26

God meets our needs
in unexpected ways.

Janette Oke

Your father knows what you need
before you ask him.

Matthew 6:8 NIV

$\mathcal{W}$e can't all leave a prestigious
background or lots of money to our children,
but we can leave them love and self respect.

Naomi Rhode

$\mathcal{O}$CTOBER 27

OCTOBER 28

Children are unpredictable. You never
know what inconsistency they're going to
catch you in next.

F. P. Jones

$\mathcal{E}$ach day is a treasure box of gifts from God, just waiting to be opened. Open your gifts with excitement. You will find forgiveness attached to ribbons of joy. You will find love wrapped in sparkling gems.

Joan Clayton

$\mathcal{O}$CTOBER 29

OCTOBER 30

Learn the wisdom of compromise, for it
is better to bend a little than to break.

Jane Wells

*T*rain a child in the way he should go,
and when he is old he will not turn from it.

Proverbs 22:6 NIV

*O*CTOBER 31

November 1

Kids are like sponges: They absorb all your strength and leave you limp. But give 'em a squeeze and you get it all back.

Barbara Johnson

$\mathcal{F}$eeling grateful or appreciative of someone or something in your life actually attracts more of the things that you appreciate and value into your life. And the more of your life that you like and appreciate, the healthier you'll be.

Christiane Northrup

$\mathcal{N}$OVEMBER 2

NOVEMBER 3

The sun...in its full glory, either at rising or setting—this and many other like blessings we enjoy daily. And for most of them, because they are so common, most [people] forget to pay their praises.
But let not us.

Izaak Walton

So much of what we learn of love we learn at home.

NOVEMBER 4

November 5

Your heavenly Father knows your needs.
He will always give you all you need from
day to day.... It gives your Father great
happiness to give you the Kingdom.

Luke 12:30-32 TLB

$\mathcal{D}$on't cry over things that were or things that aren't. Enjoy what you have now to the fullest.

Barbara Bush

$\mathcal{N}$OVEMBER 6

November 7

It is very difficult to live among people you
love and hold back from
offering them advice.

Anne Tyler

Gratitude. More aware of what you have than what you don't. Recognizing the treasure in the simple—a child's hug, fertile soil, a golden sunset. Relishing in the comfort of the common—a warm bed, a hot meal, a clean shirt.

Max Lucado

NOVEMBER 8

NOVEMBER 9

*I*nsanity is hereditary;
you can get it from your children.

Sam Levenson

I'm asking God for one thing,
only one thing:
To live with him in his house
my whole life long.
I'll contemplate his beauty;
I'll study at his feet.
That's the only quiet,
secure place in a noisy world.

Psalm 27:4-5 THE MESSAGE

NOVEMBER 10

NOVEMBER 11

*M*ost dreams take hard work and time.
You need to keep that in mind.

Janna L. Graber

If God, like a father, denies us what we want now, it is in order to give us some far better thing later on. The will of God, we can rest assured, is invariably a better thing.

Elisabeth Elliot

NOVEMBER 12

November 13

We never know the love of the parent
until we become parents ourselves.

Henry Ward Beecher

Thank You, Father, for the beautiful surprises you are planning for me today. So often in my life...an unexpected burst of golden sunshine has exploded through a black cloud, sending inspiring shafts of warm, beautiful sunshine into my life.

Robert Schuller

November 14

November 15

A mother's heart
is always with her children.

Let love and faithfulness never leave you;
bind them around your neck,
write them on the tablet of your heart.

Proverbs 3:3 NIV

Caring lifts the burden.... Courage
shoulders the weight.... But only loving
lightens the load.

Lloyd John Ogilvie

NOVEMBER 16

November 17

Who takes a child by the hand takes a
mother by the heart.

Danish Proverb

$\mathcal{B}$e on the lookout for mercies. The more
we look for them, the more of them
we will see. Blessings brighten
when we count them.

Maltbie D. Babcock

$\mathcal{N}$OVEMBER 18

$\mathcal{N}$OVEMBER 19

$\mathcal{S}$omething to be thankful for is that
you're here to be thankful.

Barbara Johnson

*B*e content with who you are, and don't
put on airs. God's strong hand is on you;
he'll promote you at the right time.
Live carefree before God;
he is most careful with you.

1 Peter 5:6-7 THE MESSAGE

*N*OVEMBER 20

November 21

Thank God for dirty dishes;
They have a tale to tell.
While other folks go hungry,
We're eating pretty well.
With home, and health, and happiness,
We shouldn't want to fuss;
For by this stack of evidence,
God's very good to us.

$\mathcal{A}$s a rose fills a room with its fragrance,
so will God's love fill our lives.

Margaret Brownley

$\mathcal{N}$OVEMBER 22

November 23

Affection is the most satisfying reward a child can receive. It costs nothing, is readily available, and provides great encouragement.

$\mathcal{G}$ratitude is a twofold love—love coming
to visit us, and love running out to
greet a welcome guest.

Henry Van Dyke

$\mathcal{N}$OVEMBER 24

NOVEMBER 25

Our thanksgiving today should include
those things which we take for granted.

Betty Fuhrman

Always give thanks to God...
for everything.

Ephesians 5:20 NCV

$\mathcal{T}$hanksgiving is a time of quiet reflection...an annual reminder that God has, again, been ever so faithful. The solid and simple things of life are brought into clear focus.

Charles Swindoll

$\mathcal{N}$OVEMBER 26

NOVEMBER 27

To tend, unfailingly, unflinchingly, towards
a goal, is the secret of success.

Anna Pavlova

$\mathcal{T}$o be grateful is to recognize the love of
God in everything He has given us—and He
has given us everything.

Thomas Merton

$\mathcal{N}$OVEMBER 28

November 29

Most of us become parents long before
we have stopped being children.

Mignon McLaughlin

$\mathcal{G}$ive generously, for your gifts
will return to you later.

Ecclesiastes 11:1 TLB

$\mathcal{N}$OVEMBER 30

DECEMBER 1

Wholehearted, ready laughter heals,
encourages, relaxes anyone within hearing
distance. The laughter that springs from love
makes wide the space around it—gives room
for the loved one to enter in.
Real laughter welcomes.

Eugenia Price

Spread love everywhere you go: first of all in your own home. Give love to your children, to a wife or husband, to a next-door neighbor.

Mother Teresa

DECEMBER 2

DECEMBER 3

Maternal love: A miraculous substance
which God multiplies as He divides it.

Victor Hugo

*F*aith makes all things possible.
Hope makes all things bright.
Love makes all things easy.

*D*ECEMBER 4

DECEMBER 5

Through the heartfelt mercies of our God,
God's Sunrise will break in upon us...
showing us the way, one foot at a time,
down the path of peace.

Luke 1:78-79 THE MESSAGE

Instant availability without continuous presence is probably [the] best role a mother can play.

L. Bailyn

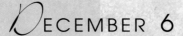

DECEMBER 6

DECEMBER 7

*W*hat we have once enjoyed we can
never lose. All that we love deeply
becomes a part of us.

Helen Keller

$\mathcal{T}$he God to whom little boys say their prayers has a face very like their mother's.

Sir James M. Barrie

$\mathcal{D}$ECEMBER 8

DECEMBER 9

$\mathcal{G}$od sends children to enlarge our hearts
and to make us unselfish and full of kindly
sympathies and affections.

M. Howitt

I know what it is to be in need, and I know what it is to have plenty. I have learned the secret of being content in any and every situation.

Philippians 4:12 NIV

DECEMBER 10

DECEMBER 11

The miracle of joy is this: It happens when
there is no apparent reason for it.
Circumstances may call for despair. Yet
something different rouses itself inside us....
We are able to remember what the sunrise
looks like.... We remember God.
We remember He is love.
We remember He is near.

Ruth Senter

Giving encouragement to others is a most
welcome gift, for the results of it are lifted
spirits, increased self-worth,
and a hopeful future.

Florence Littauer

DECEMBER 12

DECEMBER 13

To be in your children's memories
tomorrow, you have to be in their lives today.

$\mathcal{M}$ay no gift be too small to give, nor too simple to receive, which is wrapped in thoughtfulness and tied with love.

L. O. Baird

$\mathcal{D}$ECEMBER 14

DECEMBER 15

What marvelous love the Father has extended to us! Just look at it—we're called children of God! That's who we really are.

1 John 3:1 THE MESSAGE

*F*or somehow, not only at Christmas,
but all the long year through,
the joy that you give to others
is the joy that comes back to you.

John Greenleaf Whittier

*D*ECEMBER 16

DECEMBER 17

*I*t is good to be children sometimes, and
never better than at Christmas, when its
mighty Founder was a child Himself.

Charles Dickens

*G*od, being so willing to show us how to love that the Maker of the galaxies became totally intimate with a particular human body, became one of us. What greater intimacy could there be?

Madeleine L'Engle

*D*ECEMBER 18

DECEMBER 19

The magical dust of Christmas glittered on
the cheeks of humanity ever so briefly,
reminding us of what is worth having and
what we were intended to be.

Max Lucado

$\mathcal{T}$he virgin will be with child and will give
birth to a son, and they will call him
Immanuel—which means, "God with us."

Matthew 1:23 NIV

$\mathcal{D}$ECEMBER 20

Christmas is the season for kindling the
fire of hospitality in the hall, the genial flame
of charity in the heart.

Washington Irving

*L*ove came down at Christmas;
Love all lovely, love divine;
Love was born at Christmas,
Star and angels gave the sign.

Christina Rossetti

*D*ECEMBER 22

DECEMBER 23

Children need your presence more than
they need your presents.

$\mathcal{G}$od grant you the light in Christmas,
which is faith; the warmth of Christmas,
which is love...the all of Christmas,
which is Christ.

Wilda English

$\mathcal{D}$ECEMBER 24

DECEMBER 25

For to us a child is born,
to us a son is given,
and the government will be on his shoulders.
And he will be called
Wonderful Counselor, Mighty God,
Everlasting Father, Prince of Peace.

Isaiah 9:6 NIV

The most vivid memories of Christmases past are usually not of gifts given or received, but of the spirit of love, the special warmth of Christmas worship, the cherished little habits of the home.

Lois Rand

DECEMBER 26

DECEMBER 27

*H*appiness is being at peace, being with loved ones, being comfortable.... But most of all, it's having those loved ones.

Johnny Cash

$\mathcal{W}$e have been in God's thought from all eternity, and in His creative love, His attention never leaves us.

Michael Quoist

$\mathcal{D}$ECEMBER 28

DECEMBER 29

*E*ach happiness of yesterday
is a memory for tomorrow.

George Webster Douglas

$\mathcal{M}$ay the Lord continually bless you with heaven's blessings as well as with human joys.

Psalm 128:5 TLB

$\mathcal{D}$ECEMBER 30

DECEMBER 31

$\mathcal{G}$o out into the darkness and put your
hand into the hand of God. That shall be
to you better than light and
safer than a known way.

Minnie Louise Haskins